CROSS OVER INTO GAELIC WITH MAGGIE MIDGE AND THE ISLAND OF MIDGEORKA EILEAN MHIDGEORKA

by
Rab McPhee

illustrated by
Elfreda Crehan

Gaelic by Steafan MacRisnidh

Maggie's voice: Beathag Mhoireasdan

Chuidich Comhairle nan Leabhraichean am foillsichear le cosgaisean an leabhair seo.

All rights reserved. No part of this publication may be reproduced or stored in any form without permission from Lexus Ltd, except for the use of short sections in reviews.

British Library Cataloguing in Publication Data.

A catalogue record for this book is available from the British Library.

ISBN: 9781904737230

Published 2013 by Lexus Ltd
60 Brook Street, Glasgow G40 2AB

© Lexus Ltd, 2013

www.lexusforlanguages.co.uk

Printed and bound in Latvia by Inprint

In this little book Maggie tells about the island where midges go when their lives are over. It's a classic piece of ancient midge folklore.

The text is full of bridges. If you want, you can cross over the bridges and read the whole text in Gaelic.

And to hear the Gaelic spoken, you can go to **www.lexusforlanguages.co.uk** and download free recordings of Maggie's own voice.

we will fill the sky

from an old midgic chant

Is mise Maggie Midge.
My name is Maggie Midge.

Tha mi a' fuireach ann an Alba.
I live in Scotland.

Is e dùthaich bhrèagha a th' innte.
It's a beautiful country.

Leig leam innse dhut mu dheidhinn àite a tha glè shònraichte

Let me tell you about a very special place

air a bheil sinne, na meanbh-chuileagan, eòlach.

we midgies know of.

Tha àite ann
There is a place

fada a-muigh tarsaing air a' mhuir dhubh, dhomhainn
far out across the dark deep sea

seachad air na h-eileanan sgorach
past the jagged islands

fada a-null seachad air na creagan stòite
way beyond the jutting rocks

agus air na ròin reamhar mhòra
and the big fat seals

seachad air na tràighean beaga ann am bàghan beaga
past the little beaches in little bays

tha àite ann
there is a place

a-muigh, seachad air na fir ann an eathraichean
out, past the men in boats

far an saoil na faoileagan gun deach iad ro fhada
where seagulls decide they have gone too far

a-muigh, a-muigh
out, out

seachad air na h-uisgeachan far an tèid am bàt'-aiseig
past the waters where the ferry goes

agus far nach eil sgudal air fleòd
and where no litter floats

tha àite ann
there is a place

ris an can sinn **Midgeorka**.
we call **Midgeorka**.

deich millean millean
ten million million
a bha beò roimhe
who have lived before

agus barrachd
and more
fada a bharrachd
so many more

deich millean millean sgiathan beaga
ten million million little wings

sa bhloigh de dhiog
in the fraction of a second   mun caochail sinn
before we die
a nì an srann as lugha
will make the tiniest whirring noise